Whatever you do, you need courage.

Whatever course you decide upon, there is always someone to tell you you are wrong.

There are always difficulties arising which tempt you to believe that your critics are right.

To map out a course of action and follow it to the end requires some of the same courage which a soldier needs.

~ Ralph Waldo Emerson

LEADERSHIP
COURAGE

LEADERSHIP STRATEGIES FOR INDIVIDUAL AND ORGANIZATIONAL SUCCESS

WALKTHETALK.COM

Resources for Personal and Professional Success

To order additional copies of this book, or for information on
other WALK THE TALK® products and services,
contact us at

1.888.822.9255

or visit our website at

www.walkthetalk.com

LEADERSHIP COURAGE

Printed in the United States of America

10 9 8 7 6 5 4

ISBN 1-885228-60-0

Edited by Steve Ventura and Michelle Sedas
Designed by Tom Harrison and Steve Ventura
Printed by MultiAd

TABLE OF CONTENTS

INTRODUCTION

A common requirement of leaders at all levels is having the courage to make tough decisions and take difficult actions.

Courage is frequently discussed in meetings, rated in performance appraisals, and listened for in promotion interviews. Almost all would agree that it's an important element of successful leadership. Yet, becoming a courageous leader involves a lot more than talking, rating, and correctly answering interview questions.

The dictionary definition of courage is "the state or quality of mind and spirit that enables one to face danger or fear with confidence and resolution; bravery; valor." But what does all that mean in the business world? How can it be measured and quantified?

Perhaps the best way to understand courage is to define its opposite state. Some would say the antithesis of courage is "cowardliness" ... avoiding (or succumbing to) pressure, difficulty, and danger. Others would say "fear" ... being afraid to do the right thing when the going gets tough. Certainly, both of those answers are logical and appropriate. But there's another description of the opposite of courage – one not as commonly thought of, although equally valid. That description is "conformity" ... letting things be the way they have always been because of the high price associated with changing them.

As a leader, you need courage to do what needs to be done ... to do what you know is the right thing. There will always be those who tell you you're wrong – even when you're thoroughly convinced that you're right. There will always be some tempting you to take an easier and less resistant path. And, there will always be those who – either unintentionally or purposefully – create obstacles that will challenge your mettle. Even the very best leaders must regularly pass the courage test.

Courage is about having the guts, nerve, and heart to do things that foster and support progress. And that begins with the realization that: 1) improvement won't be found on the path of least resistance known as conformity, and 2) status quo is the archenemy of progress. When you think about it, "doing things the way we've always done them" requires no leadership at all. What is there to lead to? How can others follow someone who's not going anywhere? That's why "leadership" and "courage" must be viewed as synonymous concepts.

To become a courageous leader, you must have an undeniable, indisputable, and unwavering commitment to be the best you can be. The true measure of your leadership is the ability to look in the mirror and know that you had the courage to do what you felt was the right thing to do. This book will help you do just that!

In the pages that follow, you'll find eleven leadership strategies ... eleven acts of courage required for long-term success. Pay attention to them; learn them; apply them. The people you lead are counting on you. Don't let them down.

For every person in every organization, there comes a moment when he or she must have the courage to step forward and meet the needs of the time. Regardless of whether your moment is now or sometime in the future, you must be ready.

Read on, enjoy, and prepare for your time to seize the moment as a courageous leader!

 As you read this book, you'll come across our **Solution Finder**! Visit **WalkTheTalk.com** where you can immediately access our free tips to help you achieve personal and professional success!

Courage is the first of human qualities because it is the quality which guarantees all others.

~ Winston Churchill

CHAPTER ONE

The Courage to

ACCEPT RESPONSIBILITY

*One's philosophy is not best expressed in
words; it's expressed in the choices one makes.
In the long run, we shape our lives
and we shape ourselves.
The process never ends until we die.
And the choices we make
are ultimately our responsibility.*

~ Eleanor Roosevelt

Assuming responsibility can be a scary thing to do. It means we are accountable to some type of authority. We have to answer for our actions and often the actions of others. And if that which we're responsible for develops problems or fails to meet the expectations of those with authority over us, there can be negative consequences. That's why it's so tempting to avoid and shirk responsibility … that's why it takes courage to accept it.

When things go wrong, *courageous* leaders accept responsibility for their actions and the actions of their teams. *Conforming* leaders, on the other hand, typically seek and blame the person or department that created the unacceptable result. Look hard enough, and one can usually find others to blame for any situation. It takes courage to look *inside* and discover the truth that contributed to the situation.

Assembly Required

Three dreaded words that often send chills up people's spines are "some assembly required." What those words really mean is: some parts may be left over; frustration ahead; there's a chance you'll never get it put together correctly.

When you have to assemble something like a bicycle, the typical scene goes like this: You open the box and place parts all over the garage floor. You glance at the instruction book and then lay it down because "I can figure this out." Several hours later, your task is completed. The bike is together, it rolls, it looks great, and you're truly proud of your accomplishment.

Then, you look down on the floor and discover that there are a few nuts and bolts remaining. No big deal. Either someone made a mistake when packing the fasteners, or they intentionally gave you extras – in case you lose some. Nevertheless, you know you've completed the task well because your child is now happily riding down the street.

Several weeks later, the bike begins to wobble. You try to fix it, but the wheels just won't spin right – and your once happy child will not ride it anymore. That new (and rather expensive) bike becomes just another unused item taking up space in your already cramped garage. Every time you have to move that bike to get into your car, you blame the manufacturer for the problem … you're sure there must have been a lapse in quality control on the day your bicycle was produced. And you hunt through your drawers in search of the purchase receipt so you can take the obviously "defective" product back to the store.

It never crosses your mind that *you* may be responsible for the bike not working properly. But come to find out, the "extra" nuts and bolts you had left were not extras. They were needed … they would have made a difference. The person packing the parts did the job correctly and is probably a good worker. The manufacturer made a good product and had proper quality controls in all areas – except in making sure that you followed the instructions they had so painstakingly developed. Certainly, it was convenient and somewhat ego-soothing to blame others. But the real reason the bike didn't work was that YOU did not assemble it correctly – a fact that you eventually (and begrudgingly) realized. Once you accepted that fact, quit blaming others, and stopped making excuses, you were able to take the situation as it was and do something to correct it. So you called your neighbor, "Mr. Fix-it." He took the "extra" nuts and bolts and found a place on the bike for them. Amazingly, your child now has the smoothest ride in town.

Two Envelopes

Accepting responsibility is not always easy. Even though few people enjoy listening to them, the human supply of excuses is seemingly endless.

We are reminded of a story about a retiring CEO and founder who was in the process of turning over his company to his successor. After the normal speeches and kind words, the exiting executive handed two envelopes to his replacement. One envelope was marked "Number 1" – the other, "Number 2."

The replacement asked, "What are these for?"

The founder replied, "When a leadership crisis arises and you want to know what to do, open envelope number one. If another crisis comes after that, open the second envelope."

A few years later, a crisis faced the new CEO and he went to find the envelopes he had safely tucked away. As instructed, he opened the first one. It read, "Blame your predecessor!"

"That should work," thought the executive. "And it certainly should reduce the heat on me." So he followed the advice to the letter. He blamed the retired founder for the problems and voilà – the heat was off.

Many months after that, another crisis developed. Looking for a solution that worked as well as the advice from the first envelope, he opened Envelope 2. The contents said, "Prepare two envelopes!"

Blaming other people or things is never a good long-term solution. When was the last time you enjoyed hearing any of these statements: "It's not my fault" … "If they had done what they were supposed to do, I would have done what I was supposed to do" … "I was too early" … "I was too late" … "I was too busy"? You get the point.

Rights and Responsibilities

When you chose to become a leader, you entered a great profession. However, making that choice meant giving up several of the "rights" you may have enjoyed as a follower. You no longer have the right to blame others for mistakes – *you* are responsible. You no longer have the right to avoid issues – *you* are responsible. You no longer have the right to avoid decisions – YOU are responsible.

It's not unusual to hear of leaders losing their jobs because they refused to accept the responsibilities that came with the position and title. Recently, a college football coach was fired before ever coaching a game at his new school. It wasn't because of losing – no score had been posted. He was let go because he refused to accept that his coaching job came with responsibilities *outside* the yard lines. In another case, a successful basketball coach failed to recognize the responsibilities of his position and was fired – even though he won more games than anyone else in the history of the university.

A leader's responsibility cannot be avoided!

Making excuses and blaming external factors, rather than accepting responsibility, is fatal to success. There will always be excuses and others to blame for failures. But much of the time, problems come from within – from good and well-intentioned people who make honest mistakes. Therefore, you must look *inward* to understand those problems and find solutions to them.

Responsibility provides the drive to get things done. It's necessary for security and happiness. So, what are you responsible for at work? Is it the actions of your subordinates? Your boss? Your peers? The answer is that you are responsible for the success or failure of *all activities* you are associated with ... for *everything* you can either control or influence. You control setting the standards for team performance, providing feedback, solving problems, recognizing employee contributions, and a lot more.

A former president of Hyatt Hotels stated, "If there is anything I have learned in my twenty-seven years in the service industry, it's that ninety-nine percent of all employees want to do a good job. How they perform is simply a reflection of the one for whom they work." In other words, if you want to lead responsible employees, you must be a responsible leader.

In Summary

Courageous leaders avoid the temptations to fix blame and focus on the past. They opt, instead, to focus their attention on the future ... on ways to solve situations as they are. If you have the courage to take blame words out of your vocabulary and accept responsibility to move forward, there's a good chance that your team will follow your lead. When that happens, everyone wins.

To become a courageous leader, you must realize that accepting responsibility is not optional – it is mandatory. Accepting responsibility leads to confidence, self-control, and trust. And those are all qualities of effective leadership.

Success on any major scale requires you to accept responsibility ... In the final analysis, the one quality that all successful people have ... is the ability to take on responsibility.

~ Michael Korda

CHAPTER TWO

The Courage to
CREATE POSITIVE CHANGE

The only constant is change.

~ Heraclitus, 500 B.C.

When Heraclitus uttered those truly profound words in 500 B.C., do you suppose he was envisioning the warp-speed changes we face today? Probably not! Nevertheless, leading people through change in his era undoubtedly came with its own unique set of challenges and difficulties. Humans inherently resist change in varying degrees. And clearly, the message of that ancient historical figure is: Get beyond the ways of the past and present, and start looking toward improvement in the future.

There are few leadership responsibilities more stressful or difficult than implementing change. It takes courage to step away from the comfort of status quo and do things differently – and get others to do the same. Even "minor changes" can be met with passionate resistance. Yet, those minor changes sometimes can make major differences in your team's success.

Sea captains know there are many forces that control the movement of giant ships in the ocean – especially in bad weather. They have to adjust for factors like the weight of the ship, the wind, and the movement and depth of the water. But they also understand that by tweaking the relatively small rudder only a degree or so, they can alter the destination of the ship by a thousand miles. To stay on course and eventually reach the desired port, the captain continually adjusts the rudder to compensate for the external changes that are occurring.

As the leader, it's your job to steer your organizational ship. You're at the helm … you control the human rudder. External changes are driving the need for internal change. And you must constantly monitor and adjust in order to stay on course.

Why Resistance?

Why is change so difficult for many employees to embrace? Why can't people just accept that change will happen and that it can be good?

The answer to both questions is the same: Resisting change is natural. It's universal. Regardless of culture or background, humans are creatures of habit. We all have regular routines – standard operating procedures – that offer comfort and stability. Change typically represents just the opposites: UNcomfort and INstability. And few people enjoy traveling into those lands. Just ask anyone who's struggling to lose weight or give up smoking.

Besides the fact that it's natural, there are five common reasons why employees resist change in the workplace:

1. **The change is out of their control** … it represents the unknown. They didn't create it, ask for it, or want it. Who can blame them? When people feel that things are happening to them over which they have no control, stress increases and resisting behaviors are activated.

One way to eliminate that stress is to earn the team's trust long before having to work your way through a necessary change. As the leader, you must develop trust beginning on day one – preparing for the time when you ask your followers to leave their comfort zones and follow you into the unknown. Change without trust will be fought at every step, and the odds of you being successful are not high.

Many times, the change you need to implement is out of your control as well. You're asked (or told) to do something that takes you out of *your own* comfort zone. At such times, it's important to remember that your actions will have more impact on the team's reaction to change than any other factor. If you're not sold on the change, get more information. Make sure that you believe the change is the right thing to do … or, at least, voice your concerns.

Your team will eventually follow you if you believe in the change, lead with integrity, communicate consistent messages, listen to their concerns, and treat them with dignity and respect. All of those actions add deposits in your trust account, which team members will draw upon to help them through uncomfortable times.

2. **They don't understand why the change is necessary.** Without understanding the "why's" behind the "what's," emotions that are tied to the old way are hard to loosen. People have to know why they are changing before they will be willing to let go of the past. Even if they do not agree, people will accept change more readily if they understand the rationale behind it. And once you explain the reasons, create opportunities for your people to participate in the design process.

If you involve your team in determining how a change will be implemented, your chances for success improve significantly. Inform them of the options and encourage their participation in analyzing the alternatives and creating the new plan. The more people you involve in analyzing the alternatives, the more ownership of the change they will take on.

Sometimes, employee participation may not be appropriate. In those instances, you'll still want to get the team's buy-in, if possible. To do that, solicit the support of your informal group leaders before announcing the change. Ask for their involvement in delivering the message. Their visual and vocal support can make the difference in the team's acceptance of change.

3. **They succeeded the old way.** Often, there is a group of people who have excelled under the old conditions. Therefore, they don't feel the need (or have the desire) to change – even though it may eventually make them more efficient ... and make their work easier. Rarely is there a strong group of defenders of new ways to counter those in opposition. So, you can wind up with a group of strong resisters and a group of lukewarm (at best) supporters – both of whom you must lead and influence. Not an easy job!

Talk with these folks. Acknowledge their past successes. Let them know how important they are to you and the team. Tell them you need their help ... you need them to assume leadership roles in making the change happen. And talk about how the "new ways" are the "best ways" for continuing the success they have enjoyed in the past.

4. They feel incapable of changing. Rapid advances in technology can result in a fear of change. Many people lack confidence that they can keep up with new developments and therefore are threatened by them. Change is consistently resisted when people feel inadequate. Here, the leader's task is one of confidence building.

You foster confidence by actively working with your team throughout the change process. Express *your* confidence that they are up to the task. Identify past examples of when they have successfully adapted to changing conditions. Assure them that you will provide the training and support they'll need to be successful. And be sure to set the proper example. Your total commitment, and resulting actions, will be what they remember the most.

5. **They perceive that the price to pay outweighs the benefits to be gained.** Some team members may believe that a particular change is not worth the "pain" they must go through to implement it. If they don't see the "upsides" – or don't like what they see – they will do very little to make the change happen. In other words: If the benefits for *not* changing are perceived to be greater than the benefits *for* changing, people ain't gonna change (at least not willingly).

Here, the strategy is obvious: Focus on the pluses. Communicate the benefits to be gained by each member of the team. If there truly is a good reason for changing, the benefits of doing so shouldn't be hard to identify. One benefit that should always be on your list is: "Adapting to change is the very best way to protect jobs and enhance careers."

Focusing on the End

Have you ever been really late for a movie? You take your seat and catch the last ten minutes – as the hero and heroine head off to their life of happiness? All you see is the end. But you stick around – killing time until the movie starts again so you can see it from the beginning. You now watch the movie from a much different perspective. You know what happens in the end. It's locked in your memory bank. Your stress level is down; you can relax and enjoy the trials of the characters knowing that everything will be okay.

That same process is helpful when dealing with change. As you lead others through organizational changes, stay focused on the end of the story … the results to be achieved and benefits to be gained. Talk about how rewarding the desired end-state will be if everyone can let go of the past and move forward.

Positive Impacts

When you think about it, the inevitability of change is good news. Imagine what our lives would be like without the changes that flew in the face of these misguided predictions:

"Everything that can be invented has been invented."
Charles Duell, Commissioner of Patents, 1899

"Television won't be able to hold on to any market it captures after the first six months. People will soon get tired of staring at a plywood box every night."
Daryl Zanuck, Twentieth Century Fox, 1946

"I think there is a world market for about five computers."
Thomas J. Watson, IBM, 1943

"With over fifteen types of foreign cars already on sale here,
the Japanese auto industry isn't likely
to carve out a big share of the market for itself."
BusinessWeek, 1969

"There is no reason for any individual to have
a computer in his home."
Kenneth Olson, Digital Equipment, 1977

Knowing what we know now, it's obvious that these leaders were extremely shortsighted. And thank goodness they were wrong. The very things they said wouldn't happen are ones that all of us have come to rely on and enjoy. And they all were made possible by leaders who had the courage to buck conventional wisdom, abandon the status quo, and get in front of tomorrow's parade.

In Summary

The changes you lead people through today may not have a dramatic effect on the history of humankind, but they can have positive impacts on the professional lives of your team members.

It takes courage to move others out of their comfort zones and into uncharted waters. There can be resistance at every point in the process. Therefore, you have to stay at least one step ahead – always focused on the results to be achieved. Embrace change because when you stop changing, you stop improving.

At the end of every day of every year,
two things must remain unshakable:
our constancy of purpose and our
continuous discontent with the present.

~ Robert Goizueta, Coca-Cola

CHAPTER THREE

The Courage to

HIRE AND PROMOTE THE BEST

Love is blind, but hiring shouldn't be.

~ Unknown

"You can pay in the beginning, or you can pay in the end ... with interest!" There's great truth in that old saying – and its relevance to leadership comes through loud and clear when you look at the functions of hiring and promoting.

One (of many) things that all leaders have in common is the desire to fill new or vacant positions with good people. What isn't all that common, however, is the amount of effort, energy, and yes, **courage** devoted to selection processes. Hey, we're all busy. Of course we need to fill slots. Sure staffing is important. But our platters are usually full. And the temptation is great to either rush through hiring and promoting activities or to select "the next person in line" rather than taking the time (and following the steps) necessary to identify the best people for the jobs. That's no problem if you're blessed with a lion's share of luck and good fortune. But if you're like most, there's a good chance that, down the road, you'll end up spending a ton of headache-producing time trying to fix the people problems that typically result from rushed selections. That will require a different kind of courage – the gut-wrenching kind.

The Traps

Effective leadership is about standing firm ... about never lowering one's standards just to fill a position. The longer a job is open, the more pressure there is to fill it – and, therefore, the more courage it takes to wait until the right person is found.

Some leaders are swayed by internal pressures to select the "popular candidate" ... the one who is "liked" (often for all the wrong reasons). Other leaders are guided by "anybody is better than nobody" mindsets. Both approaches are expedient and may have some validity in the short term. But, if you yield to those temptations, the long-term consequences could be devastating.

Here's one you can take to the bank: The hiring decisions you make are more important than the leadership techniques you demonstrate. Think about it. You can be a hard-working, conscientious leader with well-honed skills – but if you have the wrong people on the team, you will eventually fail. Ever heard the well-worn mantra, "This company's greatest assets are its people"? That statement simply isn't true. Only the RIGHT people are an organization's greatest assets. Having the wrong people on your team will be your greatest liability. They drag the entire team down ... and create more work for you.

The Obstacles

Hiring the right people can be tough and tedious work. That's compounded by the fact that most leaders are not well-trained in the art of interviewing. Doing it right definitely requires skill, practice, patience, and courage. But, the average leader hires or promotes fewer than five people a year. How good can you be at a process you engage in so infrequently? In an 1823 letter to John Adams, Thomas Jefferson wrote: "No duty the executive has to perform is so trying as to put the right person in the right place." The same words hold true today.

Perhaps the most common obstacle to getting the right person in the right job is limited time. As a leader, you probably have more work to do than time to do it in. And when you need to hire or promote someone, you undoubtedly need him or her RIGHT NOW! If there are no great candidates in the pool, your choices are: 1) leave a needed position unfilled, or 2) bring on someone who isn't qualified. It's a tough call. Many leaders succumb to the pressure of "I have to have a warm body now." They quickly discover that the long-term pain of having hired the wrong person overtakes the short-term relief of filling the position. Fact is, the lesser of two evils is still an evil! Don't compromise to fill a position – you *will* pay for it later.

With few exceptions, the more effort you put into hiring and promoting, the less effort you need to devote to managing the performance of the people you bring on. The trade-offs are obvious ... the choices are yours. And you have to live with (and deal with) the results of those choices.

What You Can Do

Here are ten ideas and strategies to help you hire the best – even when you are experiencing the stress that comes with having a vacant position:

1. **Draw a line in the dirt.** Refuse to hire individuals who haven't behaviorally demonstrated a commitment to values such as integrity, responsibility, respect, etc. Don't fall into the "belief trap" – believing (or hoping) that you can train for these characteristics at some later date. It rarely happens.

2. **Hire people for *who* they are.** One of the biggest mistakes most employers make is to value previous work experience above all else. In today's rapidly changing world, however, experience is "how it used to be done." When hiring people, look for traits like hard-working, good team player, dependable, honest, etc. – rather than just an inventory of skills they acquired in previous employment.

3. **Hire for *tomorrow's* job.** Don't just hire for a position, hire for the future. Jobs, technologies, and markets are changing faster than ever. Hire people who are intelligent, quick learners, and adaptable to change.

4. **Use targeted team interviews.** Have multiple interviewers each focus on evaluating different applicant factors and characteristics. Divy-up things like work history, technical skills, teamwork, enthusiasm, honesty, and ethics among the interviewer group.

5. **Bring on people who are *different* from you.** You don't need anyone else to think what you think and do what you do. You're already there! Look for fresh and different people who will bring fresh and different ideas. Hire for diversity.

6. **Rate the answers, not the applicant.** Conclude the interviews feeling good about one person? Ready to make an offer? Go over your notes and pretend that a candidate you don't like as much gave you the same responses. Are they still good answers?

7. **Keep your ears open for *We's*.** Listen for the "we" word ... unless you are looking for an "I" person. One trait of good team players – no matter their level or function – is the use of the word "we" when describing previous work situations and achievements.

8. **Think long term.** Never take a hiring decision lightly. Whomever you hire today will determine what your organization will be tomorrow.

9. **Keep it legal.** The last thing you need is a lawsuit. The easiest way to determine whether a potential interview question is discriminatory is to ask yourself: "Is this question directly related to the person's ability to do the job?" Race, religion, national origin, marital status, age, disability, Workers' Compensation, and injury information are all protected. Whether or not the person has children or dependents has no bearing on his or her ability to do the job. The safest and best route is to contact your HR department and request any available guidelines for interview procedures.

10. **Do a "post mortem."** Each time you conclude your hiring activities, gather all involved staff and evaluate the process. How pleased are you with the overall outcome? What worked well? What didn't? What can you do to make the process just ten percent better next time? Consider asking new hires for their input. And once you've collected this information, ACT ON IT.

In Summary

When you have an open position, look upon that challenge as a great opportunity. Surrounding yourself with extraordinary talent is not just an important part of your job – it's also critical to your success! You have the ability to make a tremendous difference in the make-up and performance of your team. Have the courage to "hire tough" so that you can "manage easy" … and reap the other rewards that come with it.

FREE... How to Hire and Promote the Right People.
Go to www.walkthetalk.com

If you want to make a silk purse out of a sow's ear,
it helps to start with a silk sow.

~ Steve Ventura

CHAPTER FOUR

The Courage to

KEEP THE MAIN THING THE MAIN THING

*I have found that the greatest help in meeting
any problem with decency and self-respect
and whatever courage is demanded,
is to know where you yourself stand.
That is, to have in words what you believe
and are acting from.*

~ William Faulkner

One of the greatest challenges faced by leaders is the need to be consistent (and persistent) about the direction they provide for their teams. Inconsistency creates confusion, confusion creates unnecessary stress, and unnecessary stress typically results in poor performance. That's why it's imperative that you identify the things that are truly important and uncompromisable, and then stick with them. However, that's not always easy to do. In today's business world of competing priorities and conflicting agendas, it can be tempting to either chase tangents or merely "go with the flow." It takes courage to maintain a course – especially when that may mean sailing through rough waters and navigating necessary change.

Thomas J. Watson, Jr., founder of IBM, understood that you need unyielding corporate philosophies and beliefs in order to be successful. He said, "I firmly believe that any organization, in order to survive and achieve success, must have a sound set of beliefs on which it premises all its policies and actions. Next, I believe that the most important single factor in corporate success is faithful adherence to those beliefs. And, finally, I believe if an organization is to meet the challenge of a changing world, it must be prepared to change everything about itself – except those beliefs – as it moves through corporate life."

A Matter of Focus

Focus is defined as "directing energy toward a particular point or purpose." Certainly, there are many external factors that can make it difficult for teams to stay focused on what's important. Business is a very complex and multifaceted arena. And the more complicated that things are, the easier it is to lose focus. That's where leadership comes in … that's where YOU come in. Too often, those in the lead become the *sources* of complexity and instability rather than *solutions* to them. As a leader, you have the ability to create mammoth complexity or focused simplicity for your team.

Creating and maintaining focus for the team is at the very heart of leadership. And, to be sure, it's much easier said than done. Today's business environments demand flexible organizations – ones that are ready to adapt to changing market conditions and technical innovations. But constant changes, and the distractions that accompany them, can cause us to jump from activity to activity – often without completing any of them. After a while, we find ourselves almost completely in knee-jerk response modes. That's bad!

When leaders fail to maintain their focus (and therefore the workgroup's focus), the team lacks direction and clarity. Employees don't know where to aim … where to direct their energy and attention. Confusion and complexity increase. People don't understand how what they do ties to "the big picture." And it's difficult to keep everyone pulling together in the same direction. Under such conditions, if the team hits a target and achieves its goal (and that's a BIG "IF"), it will be because of luck rather than leadership. The problem with luck is that it's fleeting and unpredictable … and eventually runs out.

The Main Thing

One of your most critical leadership activities is determining "the main thing" for you and your team. The main thing is the one overriding point or purpose toward which all of your energy and attention should be directed. The ultimate question: If your work group was able to accomplish only one thing, what would/should that be?

Do you know what your main thing is? If you don't, it's a pretty safe bet that your team doesn't either. And even if you *do* know what it is, there's a good chance that not everyone on the team shares that knowledge. Don't believe us? Check with your employees. Ask them to identify your group's "main thing." Don't be surprised if you get a variety of responses – suggesting the need for some work on your part.

Here are five ways to ensure your employees not only know what your main thing is, but also that they work together to accomplish it:

1. **Share your vision of what's truly important** ... what you want and need your team to achieve. Don't just recite the organization's vision – that's great for the annual report, but employees need to know what's in *your* head. It should be a clear explanation of what your team's results can and should be ... and how you see that happening.

Each member of the team needs to clearly understand the expectations you have of him or her. Certainly, job descriptions and performance reviews will provide that information to a degree. But employees also need to hear – directly and specifically – what you require of them.

Never assume they know or will eventually figure it out. Explain what you need from them, and the vast majority will do what they can to deliver.

2. **Provide regular feedback** on how each team member is helping to accomplish the main thing. Do not fall into the "as long as you don't hear from me you'll know you're doing okay" trap. Again, your people need to hear directly from you whether things are going well or not.

3. **Show the team that you care.** If your group is like most, the question "Does anybody really give a flip about what we do around here?" probably comes up now and then. Everyone needs to feel (and BE) appreciated by his or her leader. In fact, being recognized for one's efforts and contributions is the number one factor leading to long-term job satisfaction. That's right … it ranks *above* money!

Spend time with your team; listen to them with a genuine interest. If you don't *show* them you care, they will rightfully conclude that you don't … and *they'll* stop caring as well.

4. **Identify and eliminate unnecessary activities** that either don't support your main thing or that block the progress and success of your people. Test all of the team's decisions and activities against the main thing. Then have the courage to stop doing the things that distract the team from accomplishing its top priority.

5. **Stay consistent.** The leader's job is to provide consistency in everything he or she does. Your actions must be consistent with your words. The performance reviews you conduct must be consistent with the coaching you have provided along the way; the reward system you have in place must reflect and acknowledge the accomplishment of important team goals.

The Tough Part

Determining what's important is actually the easy part. The tough part, the one that requires courage, is maintaining your focus – despite any challenges or obstacles that present themselves. As a leader, you must make a commitment to identify and diligently focus on your main thing. The truth is, it's usually leaders who are responsible for frequent changes in team direction and focus – not employees. If your main thing is always changing, expect nothing but frustrated employees. If you stay focused, you increase the likelihood that your team will, as well.

Maintaining a laser-sharp focus on accomplishing goals is neither natural nor easy. Without question, you will face distractions that will tend to pull you away from your main thing. That's okay as long as you quickly get back on track. Your job is to continually reinforce and communicate the main thing, hone your focus, and keep the team on target. That will help ensure your team's success – and yours as well.

*Determine the specific goal you
want to achieve. Then dedicate yourself
to its attainment with unswerving
singleness of purpose, the trenchant
zeal of a crusader.*

~ Paul J. Meyer

CHAPTER FIVE

The Courage to

COMMUNICATE TO BUILD UNDERSTANDING, SUPPORT, AND ACCEPTANCE

*Courage enlarges, cowardice diminishes resources.
In desperate straits, the fears of the timid aggravate
the dangers that imperil the brave.*

~ Christian Nevell Bovee

Have you ever noticed geese flying in a perfect "V" formation and wondered why they travel that way? Actually, they are making it easy on themselves. There are several dynamics happening at once:

As each bird flaps its wings, uplift is created for the bird immediately following. By flying in a "V" formation, the whole flock adds at least seventy-one percent greater flying range than if each of the birds was flying alone.

When a goose falls out of formation, it will instantly feel increased drag and resistance – and quickly get back into formation to take advantage of the lifting power of the bird in front.

The head goose will rotate back in the formation when it gets tired and another goose takes the lead. The geese honk from behind to encourage those up front to keep up their speed.

If you think about it, geese are pretty good leaders. They have a clear understanding of the mission, they know and show the way, they support and encourage each other to keep moving in the right direction, they willingly take up the slack when others in the group tire, and they communicate quite effectively (albeit squawking). Yes, they *are* good leaders ... and good team members, as well.

It's About Communication

Wouldn't it be great if your team consistently worked together as well as flying geese? Why don't they? Could it be they feel they're not paid enough? Do they perceive that the workplace is cramped and noisy? Maybe they think that leadership expects too much from them? Could organizational bureaucracy or politics be major demotivators?

All of these possibilities certainly are easy to imagine and rationalize. However, in survey after survey, employees place "communication problems" at the top of their frustration list. Communication? Yes, communication!

Leadership guru Peter Drucker claims that sixty percent of all management problems are the result of poor or faulty communication. But, because most leaders spend so much time and effort communicating, it's often hard for them to grasp the severity of the issue. The irony is that while so many employees are frustrated by a perceived lack of communication with those who lead them, most leaders feel they are outstanding communicators.

In a recent study, researchers asked a group of leaders to evaluate their personal communication skills. The findings revealed that ninety percent of those surveyed felt they were in the top ten percent. Do the math. Eighty percent of those leaders believe they are better communicators than they really are. Obviously, their perceptions don't match reality.

We often hear "communication is the key," or "leadership IS communication," or any number of similar catch phrases touting the importance of communication. These slogans are common because they're true. Communication *is* critical to the success of every business – it's one of the most powerful tools you'll find in any leader's "toolbox." Communication can be as tactical as posting the daily production and sales figures or as strategic (and profound) as sharing the purpose and vision of the organization.

With so much emphasis on communication, how could it be such a big problem? What's enough? How much more do you need to do? The way we see it, the answers are the same for just about all leaders: You don't need to do it *more*; you need to do it *better!* In most cases, employees don't need more information. After all, a great deal of what they receive is never read. That which is read is frequently not understood, and that which is understood is often quickly forgotten. Adding more data to that mix only compounds the issue.

"Static"

The real problem is one of quality rather than quantity. Too often, the messages being sent are not the same as those being received. There's a disconnect. The communications are filled with so much "static" that the messages are neither understood, supported, nor accepted by employees. That static appears in many forms, including: ambiguity, confusion, inconsistency, conflict, and mistrust.

What causes the static? A key factor is the proliferation of communication methods in recent years: e-mail, voice mail, meetings, conference calls, cell phones, pagers, memos, video, intranets, newsletters, etc. With so many options, leaders tend to pay more attention to *how* they're going to communicate rather than *what* they're going to say. In other words, it ends up being more about the medium than the message. As a result, most leaders mistakenly see communication as an "activity." The focus is on producing slick graphics, writing clever memos, or delivering great presentations – instead of creating commitment, passion, and enthusiasm among the employee ranks.

Furthermore, far too many leaders have forgotten the basic principle, and simple fact, that communication is a *two-way* process involving sending *and* receiving ... speaking *and* listening. Both functions are of equal importance, but both do not receive equal attention. Check this out: The average manager spends about three-fourths of every working day engaging in verbal communication. Nearly half of that is spent listening, and the average person is only about twenty-five percent effective as a listener. This means that if a manager receives a salary of $50,000, over $12,500 is paid for being an INeffective listener.

Some of the technological advances that have made communication easier have also depersonalized it. It's not enough to just put out a message and hope employees "get it." You have to follow up to be certain you connected ... to make sure the message received was the same one you intended to send.

Think "Outcome"

To eliminate static, you need to think of communication as an outcome. To do *that*, try looking at the process from the receiver's perspective. Ask yourself: "What is my desired outcome with this communication? What do I want people to think, feel, and do after receiving my message?"

At a minimum, your objective should be for others to understand your communication. But, employees can clearly understand what you are saying and still not agree or be willing to follow your direction. That's why your ultimate goal must be to build both support and acceptance ... to have receivers internalize your message ... to move them to action. You see, developing understanding is an intellectual issue; fostering support and acceptance are both emotional issues. It's like the basic difference between compliance and commitment. Which one would you rather have from your coworkers?

A leader can (and often does) make or break an organization. Most of the time, the determining factor of a leader's success or failure is not the strategy, it's the tactics ... how well the strategy is communicated and executed. Many great plans have failed because of communication breakdowns within organizations.

There are four critical dimensions of communication – all of which will help ensure that your message is supported and accepted:

1. **Build trust.** The core of communication is developing trust.

■ Clearly establish acceptable standards of behavior. Doing that will help eliminate one of the greatest stresses within most organizations: confusion.

■ Err on the side of employee fairness when there are no obvious rights or wrongs.

■ Pass the trust test by being consistent and living up to your commitments.

2. **Share information.** Knowledge is power. Equip your team with as much knowledge as you can.

■ Show each team member how his or her job fits within, and contributes to, "the big picture."

■ Communicate the "why's" behind the "what's."

■ Teach employees organizational vital signs and the business of the business.

3. **Provide feedback.** People need to know where they stand.

■ Let employees know what is required of them.

■ Regularly tell them how they're doing – individually and as a team.

■ Demonstrate by *your* behavior that their performance matters.

4. **"Walk the talk."** Employees are watching what you do. You're always leading.

- Earn the right to expect others to do things by doing those things yourself.

- Make sure your communications reflect and support key organizational values.

- Remember that EVERYTHING you do counts!

In Summary

As a leader, communication is one of the most powerful tools you have. Rather than think of it as an activity, think of communication as an outcome. Stay focused on your message. Work hard to eliminate "static." And make sure your goal is to build USA: Understanding, Support, and Acceptance.

So, what does all this have to do with courage? A lot! It takes courage to be open and honest. It takes courage to make it a two-way street rather than an autocratic monologue. It takes courage to share the power of information. And, it takes courage to pursue employee commitment rather than settling for mere compliance.

Conforming leaders assume their messages are crystal clear. They're surprised and angered when employees don't get on board. *Courageous* leaders, however, understand that everyone processes information differently. So, they put their focus on providing the information and motivation to gain support and acceptance. Which type of leader are you?

The art of communication is
the language of leadership.

~ Ellen Hubbard

FREE... Crash Course on Leadership.
Go to www.walkthetalk.com

CHAPTER SIX

The Courage to

BECOME AN EFFECTIVE COACH

Leadership is a serving relationship that has the effect of facilitating human development.

~ Ted Ward

One of your most important leadership responsibilities is helping *everyone* on your team reach his or her true potential – including those folks who, at times, may test your patience and be difficult to deal with. As a leader, you have a certain amount of authority over others ... you have power. And using that power wisely – for the betterment of others rather than merely for personal gain – takes both integrity and courage.

Ever heard the saying: "Power corrupts; absolute power corrupts, absolutely"? Well, some managers out there are living proof of it. You know them ... the ones who are in it for themselves. They think that because they're "in charge," employees should serve at their beck and call. Their primary focus is on making *themselves* look good. Obviously, these people are power abusers. Don't be one of them! You and your people will be much better served if you spend less time being a "boss," and more time being a COACH.

A Broader Definition

Some managers think that "coaching" is solely about addressing negative performance. And to be sure, that is part of it. In fact, it's such an important and vital part, you'll find an entire chapter on it later in this book. But the process of coaching involves more than dealing with performance problems. It also entails staying in touch with all of your team members and providing them with the information they need to achieve even higher levels of success. You see, every interaction with team members is a coaching occasion ... an opportunity to create a positive, productive climate by clarifying goals, prioritizing tasks, listening to ideas and concerns, teaching, and reinforcing desired behavior. Coaching begins with creating an environment where people want to be part of a winning team and then continues with specific actions geared toward making all team members WINNERS!

Certainly, it's unrealistic to believe that every employee has the potential to be the "best of the best." That's an exclusive club with an appropriately limited membership. But all team members *can* contribute at their *own* maximum performance levels. And helping them do that is really what coaching is all about. In fact, the verb "coach" comes from the root meaning "to bring a person from where they are to where they want to be." Instead of merely dictating what he or she wants done, an effective leader empowers team members to accomplish their professional (and personal) goals.

Super Stars

Most teams are composed of three performance groups. The first is a group of outstanding performers: the "super stars." That group typically comprises ten to twenty percent of the team – maybe even thirty percent, if you're lucky. You probably would like a larger percentage of super stars, but often they are promoted (up and out) to additional responsibilities ... which is the way it should be.

Your super stars earned their way into that category by being consistently outstanding performers. Don't overlook them! Even though they may not admit it, they need to be coached, recognized, and rewarded ... a lot! And the way you treat this elite group will determine the number of other team members who want to join the super-star ranks.

In some organizations, super stars become "the abused" as opposed to "the rewarded." Why abused? Because they have to take up the slack for those on the team who are not doing *their* jobs. The super stars are asked – sometimes required – to do more and more because others are doing less and less. They may even be abused because they are the most dependable people on the team.

You can probably remember a time when, as a top performer, you were given additional work because your manager was in a time crunch and needed a project completed quickly. Undoubtedly, that manager did not intend to "abuse" you, but that may have been your perception. And it may have affected your outlook and future performance.

Abuse your star performers and you run the risk that they'll gravitate to mediocrity – which is just the opposite of what you need. Your job is to raise the bottom, not lower the top!

Some managers think that super stars shouldn't be bothered … that they want and deserve to be left alone. WRONG! While they may not want or need you telling them what to do and how to do it, they also do not want to be ignored. Super stars are often people with strong personalities (and, sometimes, strong egos) who need to know that you appreciate their hard work and contributions. For them, your coaching role is one of supporter, promoter, and cheerleader. Encourage them frequently and let them know how much you appreciate the leadership roles they've assumed. Tell them how much they mean to the team. More importantly, tell them how much they mean to YOU!

Middle Stars

About fifty percent of your team members are probably variable performers. Some days they exceed your expectations – other days, they may fall a bit short of what's expected. A few of the people in this group may be new to the organization (and to your industry) and therefore lack the experience to be outstanding performers. And there will be some who just don't have the interest or motivation to become super stars. We call all the people in this group "middle stars."

As the largest segment of the employee population, the middle stars are the backbone of your team. Many are people who occasionally exhibit super-star behaviors but are inconsistent in their overall performance. They are important, "on the bubble" contributors – with the potential of becoming super stars ... or falling stars. Your ability to affect the performance of this group is critical to your success as a coach – and as a leader.

So how *do* you affect middle-star performance? Here are a few tips:

1. **Build their confidence by increasing their responsibilities.** Start small and then increase as they achieve success. Sometimes employees are unsure of their ability to excel. Allow them to discover their "hidden" talents and encourage them to exceed their own expectations.

2. **Give frequent and accurate performance feedback.** Be specific. Clearly explain what is required for them to become super stars on the team.

3. **Create a resource library of books** and tapes that provide team members with ideas on how to become the best at their jobs. Encourage middle stars to use these resources and discuss their key learning.

4. **Teach them how to set goals** to keep their performance on track. And, by all means, hold them accountable for those goals.

5. **"Catch" them doing good things, and then praise them.** The more you focus on finding the good, the more good you will find ... and the more they will do! Reinforced behavior becomes *repeated* behavior.

6. Hook them up with a super star for mentoring. An effective mentoring program provides middle stars with positive role models and encourages super stars to be even more involved. That's a good deal for everybody!

7. Create rewards that appeal to *their* personal values. Maybe you are rewarding team members in ways that you like to be rewarded – and it is not working for them. They will be happy to tell you what motivates them ... if you'll just ask.

Often, it's the "small things" you do that will inspire middle stars to become super stars – things like remembering facts about them and their family; asking their opinions on job-related matters; showing empathy when they're facing a personal crisis; taking the time to listen to them; or merely doing something special when they need a boost. These are, by the way, things that should be done with and for *all* employees.

Falling Stars

The final performance category in your team is "falling stars." This group is typically quite small, but the impact of its members' less-than-expected performance can be quite large. These employees consistently fail to carry their share of the load. In fact, not only are they not doing their own jobs, there's a good chance they're preventing the top performers from doing *their* jobs as well. This is a group that MUST be dealt with. And you'll find information for doing just that in chapter eight: *Having the Courage to* **Confront Performance Problems.**

The Universal Need

Regardless of which performance group various employees fall into, they all have something in common – they all share the need for CONSISTENCY.

All employees need to work in productive environments where they clearly understand what it takes to be successful. To create such environments, leaders must work at eliminating the inconsistencies and contradictions that too often are found in management practices.

Most folks have trouble accepting differences between what people say and what they do. Yet, many team members find themselves dealing with these inconsistencies on an all-too-regular basis. Workplace contradictions come in many forms: written performance reviews that differ from previously received verbal feedback; assignments and priorities that conflict with the organization's stated mission; preaching the importance of teamwork while, at the same time, implementing programs and incentives that actually pit team members against each other, etc. Inconsistencies such as these create confusion and mistrust. They blur the paths to success and can *de*motivate even the best of performers.

For a positive, productive atmosphere to exist, your walk (actions) has to clearly match your talk (expectations). You must have the courage to back your beliefs with behaviors – regardless of any pressures and temptations to do otherwise.

Remember that employees need clarity and consistency from their *leaders*. If your actions are out of sync with your words – if there are inconsistencies within the workplace – it will be difficult to positively affect the performance of your super stars, middle stars, and falling stars.

Coaches have to watch for what they don't want to see and listen for what they don't want to hear.

~ John Madden

CHAPTER SEVEN

The Courage to

ADDRESS INTERPERSONAL CONFLICTS

*One might as well try to ride two horses
moving in different directions, as to try
to maintain, in equal force, two opposing
or contradictory sets of desires.*

~ Robert Collier

Wouldn't it be great if every morning, when we woke up, all the squabbles that existed the previous day were gone? Life would be a lot easier – there would be fewer headaches and a lot less of a drain on our courage reservoir. Unfortunately, it rarely works that way.

Differences of opinion, and the conflicts that often come with them, are inevitable – especially in the workplace. As long as people interact in a work setting, ideas, viewpoints, approaches, feelings, agendas, priorities, and methodologies are bound to collide. Left unaddressed and allowed to fester, those problems can be devastating to team effectiveness. Definitely not good! This is one of several arenas in which a leader's character is put to the test.

Courageous leaders keep their eyes and ears open for potential conflicts between team members – addressing suspected issues as quickly as possible. *Conforming* leaders typically do just the opposite. They ignore conflicts until they become major problems. Then, they expend a lot of energy and emotion solving problems – much more than they would have if they had acted earlier on.

To be sure, we don't know a single leader who enjoys dealing with conflicts on his or her team. Each conflict is represented by two different and often contradictory opinions. And both of those opinions may, on face value, seem equally correct and valid. With no clear right or wrong positions, the task of addressing such problems can truly be daunting. Nevertheless, it must be done.

Surveys have indicated that more than eighty percent of problems encountered by organizational leaders involve interpersonal conflicts within the work group. These conflicts cannot be neglected on the premise (or hope) that they will work themselves out. They won't! People will always have issues … and leaders will always be needed to help solve them.

Molehills and Mountains

Ignoring a "molehill" does not make it go away – it just continues to get larger and larger. Ignore it long enough, and eventually it becomes a mountain that will block the path to where you are going. There's a conflict-resolution concept called the "1-10-100 Rule" (we call it the "molehills-to-mountains rule"). Loosely translated, the rule states that the longer a conflict exists without being identified and addressed, the more expensive and time consuming that conflict is to fix.

You can apply the molehills-to-mountains rule in many situations. It could be an interpersonal conflict between two team members, a billing discrepancy with your customer, a quality slippage, or a simple lack of communication. Those issues have at least two things in common: 1) they all negatively impact people and overall team performance, and 2) rather than fix themselves, they "snowball" over time.

Kevin and Tamara

Let's suppose that two employees, Kevin and Tamara, feel that they are entitled to work with a particular client. Both of them have good reasons for thinking the account should be theirs ... and both are right! However, a decision has to be made because only one person can be responsible for the account. There is now a molehill forming in your workgroup ... an issue that is important to those two individuals but not a huge problem.

You decide to ignore the issue – hoping it will work itself out. After several days, the rest of your team has taken sides. Some believe that Kevin is the right person for the client while others think that Tamara is perfect for this account. People are talking behind others' backs, and some hard feelings are starting to develop. Now the molehill is becoming a small mountain. Others are involved and emotional about how their "obvious choice" is being treated. The team is divided because of one client who has no idea of what's going on at your company. It takes **ten** times (1-**10**-100) more energy and effort to solve the problem now than it would have had you not ignored the issue up front. The whole team is becoming involved and team member perceptions must be dealt with. However, you're very busy with other things – so you let it go on a little longer.

Then, the client calls and leaves a message requesting assistance. Kevin assumes that Tamara is taking care of the person; Tamara thinks that Kevin is handling her. After all, they both have been debating for weeks about who should be managing the account. So, no one returns the customer's call and she promptly takes her business to your competitor down the street. The original molehill has just become a huge mountain. A client is lost, the team is at odds with each other, and *your* boss wants to know how you could have let this happen. The cost of resolving the conflict now is **one hundred** times (1-10-**100**) what it would have been if you had taken immediate action.

The molehills-to-mountains rule holds true, almost without exception: The longer a conflict is allowed to exist, the more costly it will be to fix.

Most of the time, the biggest conflicts we face begin with poor communication ... with not taking the time to understand or be understood. There is no valid reason for you to fall into that trap with your team. If a conflict arises, find out what's going on. Talk to the involved parties, describe the negative impact of their behaviors, clarify your expectations, and help them work through their issues. Consider taking a class or reading a book to enhance your conflict-resolution skills. Most importantly, have the courage to address issues before they become mountains for you to climb.

An old proverb states that you should "never leave a nail sticking up where you find it." When you apply this old proverb to organizational leadership, the translation is: Don't ignore interpersonal conflicts on your team. Address the conflicting situation as soon as it comes up because it will not just go away on its own.

*The significant problems we face
cannot be solved at the same level of thinking
we were at when we created them.*

~ Albert Einstein

CHAPTER EIGHT

The Courage to

CONFRONT PERFORMANCE PROBLEMS

*We must build dikes of courage to hold back
the flood of fear.*

~ Martin Luther King, Jr.

It's no secret that evaluation/performance appraisal systems aren't all they need to be for many managers, employees, and organizations. And it's not because they're unnecessary or unimportant. On the contrary, they're *extremely* important ... even vital. So why is it that these systems continue to fail? The primary reason is that far too many leaders lack the courage to be honest about their feelings and observations regarding performance problems. It is much easier to deliver a nonconfrontational evaluation that will be accepted by the employee rather than one that addresses issues that need to be resolved. That's especially true when performance discussions are limited to once-a-year "events" as they so often are.

When done properly, a performance review is a summary of prior conversations with the employee. There should be no surprises ... there's little or nothing the person hasn't heard before. The review typically involves a twenty to thirty minute meeting – which, by itself, certainly isn't enough to remedy any problems that may exist. Performance improvement is not an event – it's an ongoing process that involves communication, feedback, coaching, rewarding appropriate behaviors, mentoring employees, and helping them through some tough times. Unfortunately, those interventions don't happen as often as they should.

From the Small Screen

One of the most popular television series of recent times is *The West Wing*. In one episode, Josh – the Deputy Chief of Staff – was messing up royally. He was self-destructing. Clues of his personal problem were everywhere. He had a deep cut on his hand – which he attributed to the accidental breaking of a glass. No one believed him. He was irritable all the time and would jump all over any person who said that he was on edge. His performance was rapidly going downhill. Everyone (including his boss) let it slide. Some rationalized that they couldn't do anything to help – while others believed it was just a temporary lapse in an otherwise stellar record of service. Then, probably without even realizing it, he committed the ultimate faux pas … he did something you just don't do. He yelled at the President of the United States.

The Chief of Staff, his boss, chastised him and let him know that his behavior was unacceptable. Josh was defensive – covering for his pain. The Chief sent him to the White House psychiatrist. Unfortunately, there was little "the shrink" could do. The Deputy refused to accept that he had a problem.

When he returned from the psychiatrist, Josh turned the corner and saw his boss waiting down the hall.

"Why are you still here?" Josh asked – thinking that he was about to be fired.

"I'm just here to check on you," the Chief of Staff replied. The Deputy assured the Chief that he was fine and did not need to be checked on. He followed that by saying, "I don't need anything, thank you very much."

The Chief (a recovering alcoholic) did not fire him. Instead, he told him this story:

> A man was walking down the street and fell into a hole that was too deep to climb out of.
>
> A doctor walked by, heard the man's cry for help, wrote him a prescription, and tossed it into the hole.
>
> A police officer walked by, looked into the hole, heard the screaming, and wrote the man a ticket for disorderly conduct.
>
> A preacher walked by, heard the man's cry for help, and said a prayer for him.
>
> Finally, his friend walked by, heard his cry for help, and jumped into the hole.
>
> The man in the hole said, "That was stupid. Now we're both stuck down here."
>
> The friend replied, "Don't worry. I've been down here before. I know the way out."

If you're working with someone to bring about a behavioral change and/or solve a problem, it helps to have "been there" … to be able to personally relate to the situation. Of course, you may not have faced every situation your employees experience. Nevertheless, you can listen, coach, and direct them to others who have worked their way out of similar "holes."

Sometimes, however, despite your best efforts, nothing seems to work. You coach, communicate, listen, reinforce positive behavior – but the employee is not willing to change. When that happens, you must have the courage to "de-hire" and let him or her go.

HR Headaches

Nothing drives Human Resources personnel crazier than when a leader comes to them wanting immediate assistance with discharging an employee. In the leader's eyes, the person's performance is certainly worthy of firing. So, he or she gets a little testy when HR asks to see the employee's last few performance reviews to make sure the discharge is appropriate and defensible. Lo and behold, the employee has been performing at an exceptional level. At least that's what the reviews suggest. In fact, the last review shows that the employee the leader wants to let go was at the same performance level as another employee whom the leader recently promoted. Discharge this person? No can do … not without some major rule or law violation! The leader leaves feeling frustrated with Human Resources because they will not support his decision. Actually, HR would probably love to help in the process, but the leader did not have the courage to address the performance issue during the review process. The "record" doesn't support what the leader says – maybe even knows – are the "facts."

A Tough Job

Addressing performance issues is a difficult task for most people. Fortunately, such problems don't happen with any great frequency. However, even in the very best organizations, almost every leader will have to deal with at least one problem employee (uncooperative, chronically late, "just getting by" performance, etc.) each year.

Employees with performance issues represent only a small percentage of any team. Yet many leaders spend a disproportionate amount of their time with people in this group. That means that the other team members – the good, solid performers – are not receiving valuable coaching and other forms of attention that they need and deserve. And expending so much time and energy dealing with problems doesn't do a whole lot for the leader's job satisfaction, either.

Sometimes when a team member consistently underperforms, the leader assumes that he or she has failed as a boss. That is not necessarily true. A good leader helps employees get to where they need to be. Ultimately, however, it's each employee's responsibility to decide whether or not to become a contributing member of the team. Truth is, you can influence that decision but you can't control it.

Employees with continuing performance problems eventually will have a detrimental effect on your entire team. If you allow them to "skate by," you reinforce their commonly held belief that "the less I do, the less I'll be asked to do." And, since your team's workload only increases in those situations, your top performers will be challenged with more work in order to pick up the slack. Not a good strategy!

Most leaders have neither the training nor the experience necessary to comfortably deal with performance problems. And, since you were probably a top performer yourself, it's doubtful that you've had opportunities to learn from your own boss. Nevertheless, there will still be problems staring you square in the face, and you have to develop the courage to deal with them.

If you have established clear and reasonable expectations, provided adequate training, communicated the "why's" as well as the "what's," given each employee the freedom to succeed, and the performance is *still* below standard – you have a decision to make. You can close your eyes, live with the situation, and accept the negative impact of sub-par performance. Or, you can require proper performance – allowing the employee to quit and seek employment elsewhere if he or she refuses to make the necessary changes. Albeit difficult to confront, the latter obviously is your best choice. Your job is to communicate expectations and hold people accountable. Your *employee's* job is to live up to his or her responsibilities ... to fix the problem that is leading to below-standard behaviors and results.

FREE... 7 Ways to Minimize the Need for Performance Improvement Sessions.
Go to www.walkthetalk.com

Cutting Down the Numbers

Even though you will face occasional performance problems, here are several ways to help minimize the number of issues you will have to address:

- Hire people who have the talent, desire, and ability to do the job well.

- Clearly communicate job responsibilities and performance expectations. Confirm that everyone understands.

- Make training and continual learning a top priority.

- Regularly provide specific performance feedback. Make sure people know where you're headed and how they're doing.

- Consistently recognize and reward positive performance.

- Hold people accountable for negative behavior and performance.

- Set the example. Be a positive role model for your team. *Walk the talk!*

Just remember that *the employee* is responsible for implementing the plan to get back on the right track. If you do not hold him or her accountable for following the action plan, the behavior will likely not change. And you'll probably lose credibility with the rest of the team.

The Employee's Choice

Fact is, if the employee fails to follow the plan, he or she is making the choice to work elsewhere. Certainly, it's difficult to watch people leave your organization. It's worse, however, if someone has already "mentally quit" and you allow him or her to stay.

Regardless of the reason for it, being discharged is never easy to accept. The person may not understand how or why they were not meeting expectations – despite your best explanations. Your emotions will be involved ... the employee's emotions will be involved. There's likely to be disagreement – perhaps even harsh words. You'll need to be determined and prepared. Part of your preparation should always involve consultation with Human Resources. And, once you're sure that discharge is appropriate, you must muster the courage to do what needs to be done.

Here's the good news. In a survey (Clayton Sherman, Leadership House, Inc.) conducted one year after discharge, eighty percent of the former employees reported that the separation was "the best thing that ever happened to me." As unbelievable as that may sound, many discharges force people to move from a job that isn't right for them to something more aligned with their talents and interests. With few exceptions, it's also the best thing for the remainder of their team ... and the leader.

He who loses wealth loses much;
he who loses a friend loses more;
but he that loses his courage loses all.

~ Miguel de Cervantes

CHAPTER NINE

The Courage to

BE OPTIMISTIC

A pessimist is one who makes difficulties of his opportunities; an optimist is one who makes opportunities of his difficulties.

~ Reginald B. Mansell

Some people think that optimism is about living in a Pollyanna world where everything is nice and bad things never happen to good people. Well, nothing could be further from the truth. Optimism really is a courageous state of mind – one that comes from a person's desire, effort, and choice to accept and make the best of difficult situations. Certainly, the road of optimism is not without its potholes. And that's especially true for those in leadership positions.

If you serve as a leader long enough, you'll undoubtedly come face to face with setbacks and unexpected events that have the potential to be devastating. People and situations change, and your ability to remain optimistic will surely be tested against fear of the unknown. Refusing to engage in the all-too-common "woe is me" lament takes courage.

The optimistic leader believes that defeat is a temporary setback – isolated to a given situation. He or she wants the best possible outcome and therefore concentrates on finding something positive and hopeful in what appears to be a hopeless situation. This is a leader who understands a basic principle of human nature: You usually see whatever it is you are looking for.

There is an endearing story about how optimistic people look at situations differently – seeing the potential that others fail to realize. It goes like this: Two researchers were independently dispatched to one of the world's least developed countries by a large shoe manufacturer. Their task was to assess the business possibilities within that country.

When the first report came back to the manufacturer's headquarters, the message read: "No market here. Nobody wears shoes!" A few days later, the second report came back from the other researcher. It read: "Great market here. Nobody wears shoes!"

Beyond Theory

The proposition that optimism leads to success is not just theory, it's a research-based fact. Martin Seligman, a psychologist at the University of Pennsylvania, has proven that optimists are more successful than equally talented pessimists – in business, education, sports, and politics. In one experiment with Metropolitan Life, he developed a survey (the Seligman Attribution Style Questionnaire) to sort the optimists from the pessimists when hiring sales personnel. The performance of both groups was then monitored and tracked. The results were very revealing: optimists outsold pessimists by twenty percent the first year and fifty percent the following year.

Optimism increases energy and helps teams focus on long-term goals. It can be a key contributing factor to the success of any business in any industry – and an important attribute leading to leadership effectiveness. Successful leaders typically have and demonstrate the courage to remain optimistic and search for the best – even in times of stress and uncertainty. They refuse to waste their energy fretting about circumstances over which they have no control; they approach each situation with positive determination and contagious enthusiasm.

Three Keys

There are three keys to maintaining optimism as a leader. The first of those keys is **attacking worry with purposeful action.**

One of the greatest enemies any leader will ever face is worry. Worry creates fear, drains your energy, damages your health, consumes your thoughts, prevents you from achieving your potential, and obstructs your team from accomplishing its goals. Not much good can happen when you're paralyzed with fear. A leader consumed by worry cannot do his or her job effectively ... period.

Many years ago, a research study asked people to identify what worried them – and then tracked what happened to those worries over time. Here are some of the key findings:

- 40% of the worries concerned things that never actually happened.

- 30% of the worries concerned things from the past that could neither be changed nor otherwise influenced.

- 12% were needless worries about health.

- 10% were petty worries about unimportant things.

- Only 8% of the worries concerned anything substantial.

- Only half of the 8% (4%) involved things that could be controlled and/or changed.

According to that study, only eight percent of our worries are truly legitimate – and half of them are things that we can affect in some way. Even when we can't control the outcomes, we can control how we react to situations ... and what we DO to keep worry from paralyzing our teams and ourselves.

The best antidote to worry is ACTION – doing whatever we can to minimize the chances that what we fear will actually happen. Through action, we free ourselves from the "victim mentality" that can paralyze even the best of teams.

Here are some tips that can help:

1. **Get the facts.** Most worry is based on false assumptions. Get the real facts, and don't let your energy be drained by invalid or unsubstantiated concerns.

2. **Think about the worst-case scenario.** Ask yourself: "What's the absolute worst that could happen if this worry comes to pass?" Many times, you'll discover that situations aren't as bad as you originally thought. Understanding the legitimate ramifications of issues helps you keep them in perspective. And, it cuts down the number of concerns that compete for your attention.

3. **Develop action plans.** Try to improve the potential negative outcomes for legitimate worries. Create plans geared toward ensuring that worst-case scenarios don't happen. Involve everyone on your team

in plan development and implementation. It's less likely that you'll be paralyzed by worries that you're energetically working to improve.

4. **Let it go.** If you've done everything you can to prevent the worry from happening, let it go! Focus your energy and attention on other issues. Excessive worrying is counter-productive. It's an unnecessary waste of energy and emotion that's probably making you and those around you miserable.

The second key to keeping an optimistic outlook is **surrounding yourself with positive people.**

Negative people on your team can destroy morale faster than any action of a competitor. One negative person has the ability to influence scores of others. For whatever reason – and as unfair as it seems – a negative person has a far greater influence on others than a positive, optimistic person does. He or she can drain energy, destroy confidence, create conflict, hamper innovation and initiative, and reduce overall productivity. You've seen it. A new idea is developed and everyone is excited. Then, Mr. or Ms. Negative deflates everyone's balloon by saying, "Yeah, but" – and proceeds to tell you why the idea won't work. Thanks a lot! There are plenty of people who can give you "yeah, buts." Let them work for your competitors. Surround yourself with the ones who will tell you, "Yeah, and here's how we can do it."

Those of us who are parents tend to be protective and concerned about our children's chosen friends. Rightly so. We know that one of the most important decisions our kids make is choosing the right people to be around. Good friends with similar values build each other up and keep each other out of trouble. Associating with the wrong kids can eventually lead to some very difficult choices that we don't want our children to make. We want them to be around energetic, positive people. The same is true for our workplace teams.

The more you enjoy the people at work, the more you will enjoy your work. Positive people will create energy and help you figure out ways to succeed. According to many stress consultants, the secret to managing tension is to surround yourself with positive, productive people.

The third key to becoming an optimistic leader is **continually looking for the best in others ... and yourself.**

Businesses rely on and reward people who fix things. As a consequence, it's natural to be on the lookout for what's wrong ... what's broken. That, however, can be problematic. It can lead to spending the majority of our time focusing on negatives in situations *and* people. As stated earlier, we tend to see whatever it is we're looking for. So if we look for negatives in others, that's what we'll see – and we'll miss the good things that people have to offer. Effective leaders understand this. They make a special effort to focus on the best in employees. In doing so, they build a more positive working environment and increase the likelihood that team members will do even more of the good stuff.

There are times, however, when being positive runs counter to human nature. That's especially true when it comes to how we view ourselves. We *can* be our own worst enemies – looking far more critically at ourselves than most others ever would.

In general, people tend to be more careful of what they say to others than what they say to themselves. Studies have shown that as much as ninety-five percent of all "self-talk" is negative: *I can't … I won't … I'm not smart enough … I'm not creative …* etc. Should you feel that way about yourself? Absolutely not! You are not inferior to anybody. Everyone has special abilities, talents, and gifts. The faster you accept that you're okay, the sooner you'll be able to experience greater satisfaction in your leadership role.

Even when you feel pressure and stress, it's imperative to maintain a positive attitude by being a champion at positive self-talk. It *will* make a huge difference in your ability to effectively lead others. How you choose to react to whatever life throws your way determines your ultimate happiness.

In his essay *The Window*, G. W. Target tells the story of two men confined to hospital beds in the same room. Their friendship developed over months of conversation. They discussed a myriad of subjects from family, to jobs, to vacations – as well as their own personal histories.

Neither man left his bed, but one was fortunate enough to be next to the window. As part of his treatment, he could sit up in bed for just one hour a day – at which time he would share his observations of the world outside with his roommate. Using very specific terms, he described the beautiful park he could see – with its lake and the many interesting people spending their time there. His friend began to live for those wonderful descriptions.

After one particularly fascinating report, the man away from the window began to think: "It's not fair that my roommate gets to see everything while I can see nothing." He was ashamed of his thoughts. But he had quite a bit of time to think, and he just couldn't get the concern out of his mind. Eventually his thoughts began to take their effect on his health, and he became even more ill – with an unhealthy disposition to match.

One evening, his roommate – who sometimes had difficulty breathing – awoke in a fit of coughing and choking. He was unable to push the call button to get help. The frustrated, sour man lay there looking at the ceiling. He listened to the struggle for life next to him and did nothing.

Early the next morning, the day nurse came in and found that the man by the window had passed away. After a proper interval, the roommate who was so eager to see outside asked if he could be moved next to the window. His wish was quickly granted. As soon as the room was empty, the man struggled up on his elbows to look out the window and fill his spirit with the sights of the outside world. It was then he discovered that there was no park … no lake … no people. The window faced a blank wall.

This story illustrates that happiness and the ability to remain optimistic will never be achieved merely by obtaining what we perceive others to have. We *choose* our personal perspectives and outlooks based on our ability to be thankful for our own situation … whatever it may be.

Being an optimistic leader is *not* easy. It requires constant "focus on re-focus." The people on your team have personal problems, financial issues, concerns about children, and plenty of other distractions. And you have your own distractions as well. But remember that a pessimistic, cynical, negative leader will always bring disaster. Consistent, positive results are achieved only through consistent, positive leadership. Have the courage to stay focused on your goals and remain optimistic – regardless of what is going on around you.

 **FREE**… Questions That Empathetic Leaders Ask.
Go to www.walkthetalk.com

Courage is a special kind of knowledge: the knowledge of how to fear what ought to be feared and how not to fear what ought not to be feared.

~ David Ben-Gurion

CHAPTER TEN

The Courage to

BECOME THE BEST YOU CAN BE

Man cannot discover new oceans unless he has the courage to lose sight of the shore.

~ Andre Gide

Leaders who choose to rest on their knowledge – those who are not committed to personal improvement – are doomed to fail. It's that simple ... there's no other way to put it.

In today's fast-paced and constantly changing global economy, leaders who aren't growing quickly fall behind their peers in terms of skills, knowledge, and experience. These are people who fail to realize that complacency is the root of mediocrity. They become stuck in the status quo – having neither the desire nor the courage to step out of their "comfort zones."

Comfort zones are places where people are so accustomed to their situations, surroundings, skills, and routines, that any change – even one for the better – is resisted. Comfort zones are safe, predictable, and stable environments. They're filled with people who refuse to invest time and energy in personal improvement ... people who are eventually surpassed by others willing to make ongoing development a priority.

Courageous and successful leaders know, and act upon, a fact that average leaders fail to grasp: Your "comfort zone" is the number one obstacle to fulfilling your true potential.

If you desire long-term success – whether in your professional or personal life – you've got to step into the unknown and commit to being a life-long learner. The pain of tomorrow's squandered opportunities lasts far longer than the pleasure of today's complacency. Don't miss your chance!

The good news is that you have the power, right now, to make changes that will help ensure your future success. What kind of changes do you need to make? What areas or skills can you improve upon that would further your career (or just get you back up to speed)? What do you need to do to stay in the game … and win?

Taking Action

First, **set some specific goals for improvement.** Don't merely talk about personal development, DO IT! Talk is cheap. Identify some ambitious yet attainable goals, devise a plan to make them happen, and then start working your plan.

Sadly, many people today don't have clearly defined goals to pursue. How can you expect improvement if you don't know what you want to accomplish? Success is rehearsed long before it "suddenly appears," and the rehearsal begins by identifying targets to aim at. "But I don't have much experience at setting goals," you say. Well, make learning it your *starting* goal. There are plenty of resources available online and in bookstores to help you learn the goal-setting process.

Second, **dump any "personal baggage" that you may be hauling around.** Too often, leaders fail to move forward because they can't seem to let go of the past.

A few years ago, one of our associates and his wife made the decision to take only two bags (carry-on) on any airplane trip – even overseas junkets. Although changing habits was somewhat difficult at first, that decision has provided them a great deal of enjoyment and freedom as they have traveled. They never worry about losing their luggage; they never have to wait at the carousel when they arrive – hoping that the bags will as well. They're able to begin vacations an hour or so sooner. Fact is, they rarely miss having any of the unnecessary items they would be hauling around if they had more suitcases. They've learned to lighten their load ... to ease their past self-inflicted burdens. And their trips are more satisfying because of it.

If you're carrying around old baggage from past decisions, circumstances, or events, GET RID OF IT! It's stressful. It weighs you down and keeps you from doing what you want to do. If you need to forgive someone in order to eliminate the extra load you're carrying, do it. If you need to ask someone to forgive *you*, go ask him or her. The faster you rid yourself of any emotional baggage, the faster you can get ready to move onward and upward.

Third, **continue to improve by reading more.** Just because you've "made it" to a leadership position doesn't mean that your learning has peaked or ended. Just the opposite – it's only just begun. You're now challenged to learn more rapidly and share that learning with others.

The only way you can continually improve is to take in more information – about leadership in general and your industry in particular. In order to be a good *leader*, you need to be a good *reader*. Read what others are saying about your field. Get some tips; try different methods. You'll quickly discover that most of the leadership challenges you encounter are not unique. Others have traveled those roads before. Why not use their knowledge and experience to enhance *your* effectiveness?

Most people in business do not read business books with great regularity – even though doing so could provide them the information they need to become more successful. After all, reading takes time and discipline – two commodities that often are in short supply. As a result, leaders typically approach *new* tasks and challenges with *old* (i.e., "dated") knowledge and skills.

Groundhog Day is a classic comedy starring Bill Murray. In the movie, Murray repeatedly wakes up at the exact same time on the exact same day. Every day is the same "Groundhog Day" – which he lives over and over again. That script not only makes for good humor, it also depicts how many ineffective leaders approach their jobs. They rise at the same time, head for work, slide into their comfort zones, and then do little more than relive the previous day. Don't join that cast!

Did you know that you could be in the top one percent of all readers just by reading one book a month? A book a month roughly equates to half a chapter a day – just ten to fifteen minutes, seven times a week. That's doable for anyone. And, it offers an incredible return on your investment. Think about it. You can be in *the* top percentile if you have the courage and discipline to dedicate a handful of minutes each day to learning more about your chosen profession. What a deal!

Fourth, **become a mentor and teach others.** Your legacy will consist primarily of the knowledge and experience that you give to others on your team ... and, of course, the positive example you set for them.

Unfortunately, many team members do not have mentors, teachers, or even positive role models at work. In one recent study, eighty-six percent of the employees surveyed said that they could not identify one person who was a role model they wished to emulate and learn from. What a tragedy!

As a leader, you have the opportunity to have a tremendous positive impact on your team. Most people want to work for the best so they can grow and achieve their goals. Take the time to teach others what you know. They'll be better off, and so will you.

In Summary

One of the keys to a fulfilling life is having the courage to be a lifelong learner. School is never out for the successful leader. The more you learn, and the more you pass that learning on to others, the greater your chances for a prosperous and satisfying career. As the Army recruiting slogan says: **Be all you can be!**

Develop a passion for learning.
If you do, you will never cease to grow.

~ Anthony J. D'Angelo

CHAPTER ELEVEN

The Courage to

CREATE A CULTURE OF ETHICS AND INTEGRITY

With courage you will dare to take risks, have the strength to be compassionate and the wisdom to be humble. Courage is the foundation of integrity.

~ Keshavan Nair

It's no secret that ethics has quickly become one of today's most critical business concerns. Read the paper, watch the evening news, scan trade publications or legal journals and you find more than ample evidence that there are some serious problems out there. And you must help ensure that your organization isn't caught up in them – especially with the stakes being as high as they are.

Setting the Example

You have no choice about being a role model for your team. You are one ... it comes with the job. The only choice that you have is *which role* you will model.

As the leader, you have a strong influence on the thoughts and behaviors of your employees – perhaps much stronger than you think. And one of your most critical leadership responsibilities is to model the behavior you expect from others. To do otherwise is hypocrisy. You must *earn* the right to expect employees to perform with integrity by having the courage to become an ethics champion, yourself.

Your team members know they don't work for "the company," they work for *you*. They look to you – and *at* you – for guidance and direction. And just as you have expectations of them, they have expectations of you. They expect you to be honest, fair, competent, caring, and committed. They expect you to be a steward of your organization's values. They expect you to walk the talk ... to have the courage to do the right thing regardless of temptations to do otherwise. They expect all of that, and more ... they *deserve* all of that, and more.

Ethical business practices are not the responsibility of leadership alone. Performing with integrity is every employee's duty. But it must (and does) begin at the top. You are, after all, leading the way. And for better or for worse, where you lead, employees will follow.

Getting Everyone "On Board"

For ethics and values to "happen," employees must be motivated to step up and take action. Leaders produce that motivation by: 1) having the courage to avoid discouraging behaviors, 2) holding everyone accountable for performing with integrity, and 3) "doing right" by those who do right!

Behaviors That Discourage

Here are twelve ways a leader can discourage trust, integrity, and ethics in his or her work unit. **Avoid these at all costs:**

1. Promoting an employee who does not have the trust and respect of coworkers.

2. Professing verbal support for an "Open Door Policy" while behaviorally discouraging its use.

3. Hiring an employee without making sure that he or she has "walk-in" ethical beliefs and a history of ethical behaviors.

4. Failing to confront "small" integrity breaches because of competing priorities, poor coaching skills, or "it just doesn't matter" justifications.

5. Talking about people "behind their backs" – and allowing others to do the same.

6. Demonstrating power and control by withholding information.

7. Not considering the organization's shared values when making decisions.

8. "Bad mouthing" the organization and blaming others.

9. Using ethnic, gender, or other "those people" slurs and negative references.

10. Not preaching, teaching, and supporting the organization's mission, vision, values, and ethical standards.

11. Failing to listen to the ideas and suggestions of others. Worse yet – asking for input but ignoring the information.

12. Not understanding the universal ethics principle: Ethics is displayed in everything we do ... EVERYTHING counts!

And to make a baker's dirty dozen – the number one way a leader can discourage ethical beliefs and behaviors:

13. **FAILING TO WALK THE TALK!**

Holding Everyone Accountable

Here's a question to ponder (it won't take long): What in our adult world, that's truly important, has no associated accountabilities or consequences? The answer is NOTHING!

Fact is, importance and accountability go hand-in-hand. It's important to pay taxes – and we're accountable for doing so. It's important to obey the laws of the land – and we're accountable for doing so. And when it comes to ethics and integrity, it's important to consistently do the right thing … and we all MUST be held accountable for doing so! You make that happen by backing up words (stated expectations) with actions. And that's another critical responsibility of leadership.

There are two performance end-states that cannot be tolerated in any organization: not getting results and *getting* results the WRONG way. In today's competitive world, it can be far too easy to jump all over the first one while letting the second one slide. Muster the courage to fight such temptations! Regardless of the state of the economy – despite the need for profit and expediency – the ends still do NOT justify the means. As a leader, you must hold people (and yourself) accountable for achieving results *the right way*.

Ultimately, holding people accountable means refusing to condone improprieties – regardless of the source. You must respond quickly and thoroughly to all unethical behaviors you see or hear about. Your first priority: Take immediate steps to correct the situation and stop any inappropriate behavior. Then, conduct a thorough investigation – collecting all the facts. Finally, deal with the offender(s) according to your organizational procedures and guidelines (after acquiring necessary counsel from the proper sources).

"Doing Right" by Folks

It's one of the basic principles of behavioral science: Reinforced behavior is repeated behavior.

From early childhood, we learn to seek, do, and replicate actions that bring positive consequences. We also typically avoid actions that result in negative consequences and eventually ignore those that produce no consequences at all. These tenets are directly relevant to organizational ethics, and they need to be at the core of your leadership activities.

What happens when people on your team perform with integrity – which might include challenging the appropriateness of an organizational action or practice? Are they given support and encouragement for their behavior? If the answer is *yes*, congratulations! You're doing right by those who do right and contributing to a culture of trust and values-based business practices. But if the answer is *no*, you're exposing yourself to:

- An unwillingness of coworkers to bring any ethical dilemmas they face to you.

- The inability to attract and retain high-integrity employees.

- A "slippery slope" of unethical attitudes and behaviors.

- Misconduct and the resulting legal liabilities.

- Loss of customer confidence and marketplace reputation.

- Reduced pride, professionalism, and overall performance.

Here's one you can take to the bank: **Ethical leaders appreciate ethical employees doing ethical things.** And they demonstrate that appreciation by recognizing (even celebrating) people who show the "right stuff" when it comes to integrity.

*To see what is right and not to do it
is cowardice.*

~ Confucius

CLOSING THOUGHTS

Effective leaders share many characteristics. Perhaps the two most important of those characteristics are: 1) having the courage to make tough decisions, and 2) being willing to make personal sacrifices for the benefit of others.

Over two thousand years ago, Alexander the Great led his troops across a hot and desolate plain. After eleven days of a grueling advance, he and all the soldiers were near death from thirst. They pressed on, however, into the twelfth day.

At midday, two of his scouts brought Alexander what little water they had been able to find. It hardly filled a cup. His troops stood back and watched – expecting him to drink. Instead, he poured the water into the hot sand. When questioned on his action, he said, "It's of no use for one to drink when many thirst." Alexander gave his followers the only things he had to give at that moment: example and inspiration.

Leadership is not for the faint of heart. A career in leadership brings awesome responsibilities – along with consequences of failure that can be great and far-reaching. But few other jobs provide a person with greater opportunities to positively impact the lives of others and the corporate "bottom line." That's what makes it so worthwhile.

A leadership career offers daily challenges and tremendous rewards. However, many potentially great leaders give up and move on when times gets tough. In most cases, that's a huge mistake. The grass is rarely greener on the other side. Develop the courage and resolve to hang in there … to work through issues rather than running from them. You can make a difference!

Consider the exceptional leaders you have experienced in the past. Reflect on the positive impact they've had on your life and career. You now have that same opportunity to make a difference for the people you manage. The benefits of courageous leadership extend well beyond any financial rewards. While money is important, the true prize is the personal satisfaction you will receive from providing an environment in which others grow, develop, and flourish.

Challenge yourself to dig deep into the role of a leader. Read all that you can about management and leadership. Become a life-long learner. Strive to keep your knowledge fresh and your attitude positive. Develop and apply new skills that will not only accelerate your own growth and success, but those of your people as well.

Truly effective leaders don't get that way by accident, coincidence, or luck. They consciously *decide* to do right things – regardless of the path that others take. They possess and demonstrate the courage to:

- ACCEPT RESPONSIBILITY

- CREATE POSITIVE CHANGE

- HIRE AND PROMOTE THE BEST

- KEEP THE MAIN THING THE MAIN THING

- COMMUNICATE TO BUILD UNDERSTANDING, SUPPORT, AND ACCEPTANCE

- BECOME EFFECTIVE COACHES

- ADDRESS INTERPERSONAL CONFLICTS

- CONFRONT PERFORMANCE PROBLEMS

- BE OPTIMISTIC

- BECOME THE BEST THEY CAN BE

- CREATE CULTURES OF ETHICS AND INTEGRITY.

Doing these things will not guarantee instant success. However, if you master each of those eleven strategies, you'll be much more likely to attract and retain the best, brightest, and most courageous employees. They, in turn, will attract the very best customers – people who give their ongoing business to organizations that place a premium on service, leadership, and treating everyone with dignity and respect. And that's the competitive advantage your organization needs in order to be successful today ... and in the future.

As Theodore Roosevelt said, "We see across the dangers of the great future, and we rejoice as a giant refreshed. The great victories are yet to be won, the greatest deeds yet to be done."

Best wishes to you, as you become the courageous leader your people and your organization need you to be.

Courage changes things for the better ...
With courage, you can stay with something
long enough to succeed at it –
realizing that it usually takes two, three,
or four times as long to succeed as you
thought or hoped.

~ Earl Nightingale

ABOUT THE AUTHORS

David Cottrell, president and CEO of CornerStone Leadership, is an internationally known leadership consultant and speaker. His business experience includes senior management positions with Xerox and FedEx. David is the coauthor of seventeen books, including *Monday Morning Leadership* and *Listen UP, Leader!*

Eric Harvey is a renowned author, consultant, speaker, and president of The Walk The Talk® Company. His thirty-plus years of professional experience are reflected in thirty highly acclaimed books to include *WALK THE TALK ... And Get The Results You Want*, *Ethics4Everyone*, and *The Leadership Secrets of Santa Claus™*.

ABOUT THE PUBLISHER

Since 1977, The WALK THE TALK® Company has helped individuals and organizations, worldwide, achieve success through Values-Based Practices. Our goal is both simple and straightforward: **to provide you and your organization with high-impact resources for your personal and professional success!**

We specialize in…

- How-To Handbooks and Support Material
- Group Training Programs
- Inspirational Gift Books and Movies
- Do-It-Yourself Training Resources
- Motivational Newsletters
- 360° Feedback Processes
- The popular ***212° the extra degree, Start Right…Stay Right,*** and ***Santa's Leadership Secrets*® Product Lines**
- …and much more!

Please call **1.888.822.9255** or Visit us online **walkthetalk.com**

Introducing FREE online newsletters from WalkTheTalk.com

- **Customer Service Monday Morning Must-Read:** Practical tips to increase customer satisfaction, loyalty, and retention.

- **The Power of Inspiration:** Designed to uplift, inspire, and motivate you and the important people in your life.

- **212° Midweek Motivator:** Midweek motivation inspiring you to achieve results beyond your wildest expectations.

- **Leadership Lessons:** Weekly tips to help you and your colleagues become more effective and respected leaders.

- **Daily Motivation:** Powerful messages to "kick start" your day.

WalkTheTalk.com newsletters are designed to motivate, inform, and inspire you to reach new levels of skills and confidence! Visit WalkTheTalk.com to sign up for these powerful newsletters!

This high-impact "do-it-yourself" training program includes:

✓ Leaders Guide with instructions, learning exercises, discussion questions, and other training tips to insure your success.

✓ PowerPoint training visuals which can easily be customized to fit your audience and training objectives.

For only **$79.95**, you can train your entire team on the *Leadership Courage* key concepts. Once you order, you will receive instructions via email on how to download the complete *Leadership Courage UTrain Program*. It's that easy! Please make sure you include your email address on the order form when you order. Better yet, order online at www.walkthetalk.com and download it immediately!

ORDER FORM

Have questions? Need assistance? Call 1.888.822.9255

☑ **Please send me extra copies of *Leadership Courage***

1-24 copies $14.95 each   25-99 copies $13.95 each   100-499 copies: $12.95 each   500+ copies please call

Leadership Courage	_____ copies X $ _____	=$_____
Leadership Courage UTrain Program	_____ copies X $ 79.95	=$_____
Lead Right Library	_____ sets X $ 99.95	=$_____

(Sales Tax Collected on TX Customers Only)

Product Total	$_____
*Shipping & Handling	$_____
Subtotal	$_____

Sales Tax:

Texas Sales Tax – 8.25%	$_____
Total (U.S. Dollars Only)	$_____

*Shipping and Handling Charges

No. of Items	1-4	5-9	10-24	25-49	50-99	100-199	200+
Total Shipping	$6.75	$10.95	$17.95	$26.95	$48.95	$84.95	$89.95+$0.25/book

Call 972.899.8300 for quote if outside continental U.S. Orders are shipped ground delivery 3-5 business days.
Next and 2nd business day delivery available – call 888.822.9255.

Name_____ Title_____

Organization_____

Shipping Address_____

City_____ (No PO Boxes) State_____ Zip _____

Phone_____ Fax_____

E-Mail (required for UTrain orders)_____

Charge Your Order: ❑ MasterCard   ❑ Visa   ❑ American Express

Credit Card Number_____Exp. Date_____

❑ Check Enclosed (Payable to The WALK THE TALK Company)

❑ Please Invoice (Orders over $250 ONLY) P.O. Number (required)_____

ALKTHETALK.COM
ources for Personal and Professional Success

PHONE 1.888.822.9255 or 972.899.8300 M-F, 8:30-5:00 CST.	**ONLINE** www.walkthetalk.com **FAX** 972.899.9291	**MAIL** WALK THE TALK Co. 1100 Parker Square, Suite 250 Flower Mound, TX 75028

And to help your leaders be courageous...

The
WALK THE TALK®
360° Profile

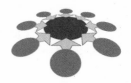

The **WALK THE TALK® 360° OnLine Profile** is an online performance feedback and development tool designed for leaders at all organizational levels. This powerful and easy-to-administer process provides performance feedback on 36 results-oriented leadership characteristics. Each participant leader receives a comprehensive 20-page personal profile along with resources to help him/her turn information into action.

This highly effective system:

- Highlights an individual's performance strengths.
- Pinpoints performance deficiencies.
- Targets developmental and coaching opportunities.
- Increases self-awareness.
- Helps align leadership performance with organizational objectives.
- Prioritizes opportunities for improvement.

Additional consulting services, training materials, and support services available.

Features and Benefits

- Unlimited number of feedback providers.

- All processed components, from orientation materials to evaluation reports, are done online.

- Easily customized to an organization's values, business objectives, and targeted leadership behaviors.

- The process is self-administered with a minimum of time investment.

- Option to have electronic or "hardcopy" delivery of individual feedback reports.

- No software to install or certification required.

Quantity discounts available.

To learn more, please contact us at
360feedback@walkthetalk.com or call **1.888.822.9255**